CHRISTMAS

Programs
for the Church

compiled by

Pat Fittro

**STANDARD
PUBLISHING**
Cincinnati, Ohio

The Standard Publishing Company, Cincinnati, Ohio
A division of Standex International Corporation
© 1995 by The Standard Publishing Company
All rights reserved
Printed in the United States of America

ISBN 0-7847-0339-6

Contents

There's Peace in the Manger

Diane Gibson

Characters
Father
Mother
Jill, their daughter
Jered, their son
Speakers—to read Scripture

Setting: The living room of a family's home

Props: A table, two easy chairs, (perhaps a fireplace backdrop or a lamp to give a homey appearance), a nativity scene, a Bible, a large shopping bag filled with packages, several schoolbooks, a newspaper, a bell, a Christmas catalog.

May use solos, a choir or the congregation for the music.

Scriptures are from *The Holy Bible, New International Version,* unless otherwise noted.

Preliminary Music

Processional Hymn: "O Come, All Ye Children" *(The Children's Hymnal,* Concordia Publishing House)

Invitation to Worship:
LEADER: The Lord gives strength to His people; the Lord blesses His people with peace.
CONGREGATION: Praise be to you, O Lord, for your blessing of peace.
LEADER: Great peace have they who love your law, and nothing can make them stumble.
CONGREGATION: Cause us to love your law, O Lord, and know your peace.
LEADER: You will go out in joy and be led forth in peace.
CONGREGATION: Lead us to walk in your peace, O Lord.
LEADER: Now may the Lord of peace Himself give you peace at all times and in every way.
CONGREGATION: We find our peace in you, O Lord. Praise be to you!

Scene 1—There's Peace in the Manger

JERED: Mom, when are we going to start decorating for Christmas?

JILL: Yes. When? I can hardly wait!

FATHER: Hold it! Thanksgiving was just yesterday. Be patient!

MOTHER: Oh dear! You know, sometimes I almost dread it when Christmas time comes around. Everything gets so busy and hectic, and it seems like the real meaning just gets lost in the hustle and bustle of it all. I just wish we could have a calm, simple Christmas for once without all the rush and activities, shopping and . . .

JERED: Oh, Mom, you don't really mean that do you? Christmas wouldn't be Christmas without all those things.

JILL: Yes, it wouldn't seem like Christmas without all the presents and decorations and parties, and . . .

FATHER: I think your mother has a point, children. It's very easy for us to get so wrapped up in all the activities that the real meaning of Christmas, the birth of Jesus, takes a back seat to everything else.

JERED: Oh, but we don't mean to do that, Dad.

FATHER: Yes, I know we don't, son, but it happens. Jesus is what Christmas is all about and all the other things seem to push Him aside.

JILL: You know, every night before I go to sleep I look at that picture of Jesus hanging above my bed. And sometimes I pray aloud and say, "Jesus, even though I forgot about *You* at times today, thank You for not forgetting *me*."

MOTHER: Jill, I think you just hit upon a great idea for us this Christmas!! I'll be right back.

JERED: Where's she going?

FATHER: I don't know, but she's got something in mind.

JILL: What did I say?

MOTHER *(returns, carrying a large box):* Here it is!

JERED: The nativity scene? But we put that up every year.

MOTHER: Yes, but this year we're going to do things a little bit differently. Let's set it up over here like we always do.
Now, Jered, please bring the Bible over here right next to the scene. We all know how easily we get frustrated at Christmas time. And we know how easily we forget about Jesus at Christmas. Well, this year I have an idea that we can all work on together.

JILL: What's the idea?

MOTHER: Well, Jill, just like looking at that picture of Jesus helps you every night, perhaps if we look at the manger scene every day, it will help us to keep our thoughts centered on Jesus and why He came.

JERED: But we've put up the manger scene every year before this and it never seemed to change things.

MOTHER: Perhaps not, but this year if we all agree to look upon it each day and think about what Jesus did, it could make a great difference.

JILL: But what's the Bible for?

FATHER: The Bible can be our special guide, too. If we remind ourselves to read something from the Bible each time we seem to lose sight of Jesus . . .

JERED: I know . . . we'll find answers in the Bible. My teacher tells us that all the time.

JILL: It's kind of like finding a peace in the manger. We'll find the peace we need by looking in the manger.

FATHER: That's it!—A real peace in the manger.

MOTHER: Is this something we all promise to do this Christmas? No exceptions?

JERED: Well, I don't think it's going to be very easy for me . . . *(long pause)* . . . well, I guess so.

JILL: Yes, I'll do it.

FATHER: It's not going to be easy for any of us. But if we do it, we will keep Jesus first this Christmas, because we'll find His peace every time we go to the manger—no doubt about it!

JILL: Yes, because Jesus will always be in that manger.

SONG: "As with Gladness Men of Old"

Scene 2—Shopping Day

MOTHER *(comes in, plops down into a chair, dropping packages)*: The shopping day blues are upon me already! Oh, I can't stand all those mobs of pushing, shoving people, traffic, long lines . . . I don't think this is what God had in mind for Christmas at all . . . but what did we say? . . . We'd find peace in the manger. *(Walks over to the nativity scene.)*
It looks so peaceful in your manger, Jesus . . . calm, quiet, still. I find it hard to be peaceful now with all the crowds and the shopping rush. Do you have an answer for me, Jesus?

(She opens up the Bible and begins to read silently.)

SPEAKER 1: "The Lord gives strength to his people; the Lord blesses his people with peace" (Psalm 29:11).

SPEAKER 2: "You will keep in perfect peace him whose mind is steadfast, because he trusts in you" (Isaiah 26:3).

SPEAKER 3: "I have told you these things, so that in me you may have peace. In this world you will have trouble. But take heart! I have overcome the world" (John 16:33).

MOTHER *(closes Bible and gazes into manger again):* Yes, Jesus, that is why You came. You came to bring peace to the world. And I can find it in You. Even amidst all the rush and busyness, I know You are here and that You love me and will give me strength. Thank You for Your peace!

SONG: "Still, Still, Still" (Augsburg Publishing House)

Scene 3—Memory Work

JERED *(comes in angrily with schoolbooks under his arm):* Oh, Mom, you should see all the stuff I have to memorize for the school Christmas program this year. My favorite TV programs are on tonight, too, and now I have to spend the whole night memorizing. I hate memorizing and I hate all the songs, too. They go so high only the girls can sing them anyway.

MOTHER: Remember what our agreement was. Go ahead—go to the manger. You'll get an answer.

JERED: Oh, Mom! Do I have to?

MOTHER: We agreed, Son. Go on, try it! *(She leaves the room.)*

JERED *(looks into the manger, starts talking to himself):* I don't think this is going to help anything. I'll still have to memorize those dumb ol' songs. *(Looks a little more closely into the manger.)* They sure make these figures kind of weird looking. Look at that sheep. It doesn't even look like one. I never did like this dumb ol' manger scene anyway. *(Yells into the other room.)* Mom!! It's not working!! *(Pauses.)* I guess she's upstairs. Well I guess I'll look in the Bible. Everybody's always making me do things I don't want to do.

SPEAKER 1: "Your attitude should be the same as that of Christ Jesus: Who, being in very nature God, did not consider equality with God something to be grasped,

SPEAKER 2: "But made himself nothing, taking the very nature of a servant, being made in human likeness.

SPEAKER 3: "And being found in appearance as a man, he humbled himself and became obedient to death—even death on a cross!" (Philippians 2:5-8).

JERED: Wow, Jesus! You sure did something you didn't really want to do. You had to come to this earth as a man and even be killed for us. That's real sacrifice! And here I am complaining about giving up some TV programs to memorize some songs. Thank You Jesus for coming and dying for me, even though it was hard.

SONG: "What Child Is This?"

Scene 4—The Tired Father

FATHER *(plops down on chair, putting feet up):* Oh, what a day! I'd just like to put my feet up and watch a little TV, read the paper a bit and fall asleep right here . . . . But, my evening's already been planned for me. I promised to help decorate the church tonight. And I forgot I promised to string the lights outside and hang the wreath. It seems like every night there's something. I'm so tired! *(Goes to manger.)* I haven't taken a look at the manger yet. I don't see where You can take away all the things I have to do, Lord, but perhaps You have some words to help me.

SPEAKER 1: "Come to me, all you who are weary and burdened, and I will give you rest" (Matthew 11:28).

SPEAKER 2: "I have come that they may have life, and have it to the full" (John 10:10).

SPEAKER 3: "But those who hope in the Lord will renew their strength. They will soar on wings like eagles; they will run and not grow weary, they will walk and not be faint." (Isaiah 40:31).

FATHER: Oh, Jesus, I can sure grumble and complain easily, but I forget that that's why You came so many years ago. You came as a baby so we could have an abundant, full life. You know what it's like to be tired because You were tired yourself at times. But You give us rest and strength when we ask. So I ask You for strength now. Thank You, Lord.

SONG: "Silent Night! Holy Night!"

Scene 5—Swaddling Clothes

JILL: Mom, can't I please have that velvet dress that we saw in the boutique yesterday for Christmas?

MOTHER: No, sweetheart, I told you that yesterday. It's much too expensive. That dress we saw in the department store is just as nice and more affordable.

JILL: Oh, Mom! You don't understand at all. Linda is getting a new dress just like it, and *her* family can afford it.

MOTHER: I don't want to hear any more about it, and that's final!

JILL: Oh!! I can never get anything I want! That dress at the other store is ugly! I wouldn't be caught dead wearing it! Why can't I have that nice velvet dress! *(She goes to manger.)* Jesus, I don't see what's so wrong about wanting something nice. What words do You have for me?

SPEAKER: "And she brought forth her firstborn son, and wrapped him in swaddling clothes, and laid him in a manger" (Luke 2:7, King James Version).

JILL: "Swaddling clothes!"—Why that's almost like rags. Boy, Jesus, You didn't have nice, warm blankets and clothes or even a cute little baby outfit. You didn't have anything like we have today. You were just wrapped in strips of cloth. And You were the Savior! The King of all the earth! Oh, I'm sorry for complaining. You were born meek and lowly for me!

SONG: "In a Little Stable" (*Little Ones Sing Praise* Concordia Publishing House)

Scene 6—Give, Give, Give!

(Ringing of a bell in the distance can be heard.)

MOTHER: Everywhere I go they're asking for handouts. Give to this, give to that. There seems to be someone ringing a bell on every corner. The church puts extra envelopes in the bulletin. Even the mail seems to have something asking for donations every day. Give, give, give! It just makes me feel all the more guilty when I don't.

SPEAKER 1: "Give, and it will be given to you. A good measure, pressed down, shaken together and running over, will be poured into your lap. For with the measure you use, it will be measured to you" (Luke 6:38).

SPEAKER 2: "Each man should give what he has decided in his heart to give, not reluctantly or under compulsion, for God loves a cheerful giver" (2 Corinthians 9:7).

SPEAKER 3: "The life I live in the body, I live by faith in the Son of

God, who loved me and gave himself for me" (Galatians 2:20).

SPEAKER 4: "For God so loved the world that he gave his one and only Son, that whoever believes in him shall not perish but have eternal life" (John 3:16).

MOTHER: Oh, Jesus! You are my perfect example when it comes to giving. You gave *me* everything! Your whole life was devoted to me. I may not be able to give to everything, but I will give what I can and do it cheerfully. Forgive me for my selfishness. Teach me to give to others as You have given to me.

SONG: "I Wonder as I Wander"

Scene 7—The Quarrel

JILL: Give me that catalog! You've been looking at it all day long!

JERED: No way! I'm not through making my Christmas list yet!

JILL: What do you mean you're not through yet? Your list is already three pages long. You'd have everything in that book if you could.

JERED: I would not! Not any more than you would want! You just want dumb ol' clothes anyway!

JILL: That's better than all those silly toys and games you want. Then you just break them anyway. Give it here!

MOTHER *(comes stalking in quickly):* That's enough—both of you! I'm sick and tired of you two arguing all the time. I've half a notion to take away both your lists and throw them away and neither one of you will get anything for Christmas!

JERED: Oh, Mom! She started it! I was just minding my own business when she came in and started bugging me!

MOTHER: I said, that's enough.

(Silence—They all stare at one another.)

JERED: Don't tell me! I know! *(He brings the Bible over.)*

MOTHER: I wonder how the Lord can put up with us sometimes, myself included. We really get nasty and upset with one another. Let's see what He has to say to us today.

SPEAKER 1: "The Lord is compassionate and gracious, slow to anger, abounding in love" (Psalm 103:8).

SPEAKER 2: "He will not always accuse, nor will he harbor his anger forever" (Psalm 103:9).

SPEAKER 3: "As far as the east is from the west, so far has he removed our transgressions from us" (Psalm 103:12).

10

SPEAKER 4: "I write to you, dear children, because your sins have been forgiven on account of his name" (1 John 2:12).

SPEAKER 5: "Be kind and compassionate to one another, forgiving each other, just as in Christ God forgave you" (Ephesians 4:32).

MOTHER: If God can forgive us, we certainly must forgive one another. I'm sorry, children.

JILL: I'm sorry, too, Jered.

JERED: I'm sorry, Jill.

SONG: "Jesus Lead Me Day by Day" *(The Children's Hymnal,* Concordia Publishing House)

Scene 8—Sorrow at Christmas

MOTHER: What's the matter, dear? You look so depressed.

FATHER: Oh, you remember Bill from the office?

MOTHER: Yes. I remember him—the one whose wife passed away recently.

FATHER: Yes, that's him. Well I just wish I could cheer him up. He is so depressed. I can certainly understand his sadness. But Christmas should be a happy time. I wish there was something I could do.

MOTHER: Well, his wife was a Christian wasn't she?

FATHER: She certainly was. She loved the Lord dearly.

MOTHER: Knowing that she is happy in Heaven should lighten his sorrow somewhat. Just think—she gets to spend Christmas with Jesus. She couldn't have any greater joy.

FATHER: Perhaps I can find some messages to share with Bill.

SPEAKER 1: "This is how God showed his love among us: He sent his one and only Son into the world that we might live through him" (1 John 4:9).

SPEAKER 2: "I write these things to you who believe in the name of the Son of God so that you may know that you have eternal life" (1 John 5:13).

SPEAKER 3: "Where, O death, is your victory? Where, O death, is your sting?" (1 Corinthians 15:55).

SPEAKER 4: "But thanks be to God! He gives us the victory through our Lord Jesus Christ" (1 Corinthians 15:57).

FATHER: Those are all certainly words of comfort and joy. You know, that is just what Christmas is all about. Jesus came to earth as a man to live and die so we could be with Him in

Heaven some day. *(Goes over to the manger.)* That's not just some baby in a manger! That's our Savior! Because *He* came, *we* have eternal life! Those who die before us just get to experience Heaven a little sooner. Isn't it great that because of this little baby Heaven is ours!!

SONG: "God Rest You Merry, Gentlemen"

Scene 9—Ponder It in Your Heart

MOTHER: You know, I have really enjoyed Christmas this year. We really have found a peace in the manger. We have felt a real closeness to the Savior. I am sad to see it all end so quickly. I wish we could keep this spirit of Christmas all year long.

(Jill comes running in.)

JILL: Hey, Mom, hey, Dad! Let me say my part for the Christmas program one more time. I want to be sure I know it.

FATHER: Go ahead. We're listening.

JILL: "So they hurried off and found Mary and Joseph, and the baby, who was lying in the manger. When they had seen him, they spread the word concerning what had been told them about this child, and all who heard it were amazed at what the shepherds said to them. But Mary treasured up all these things and pondered them in her heart" (Luke 2:16-19).

FATHER: Nice job, Jill!

MOTHER: Why, that's it! The Scriptures have given us another answer! "But Mary treasured up all these things and pondered them in her heart." That's how *we* can keep the spirit of Christmas with *us*. When we take time to ponder on those things which Christ said and did, they seem to take root in our hearts and grow. We can find a real peace now at Christmas and we can keep that peace every day of our lives.

JERED: Peace in the manger. Yep, I think we found it.

FATHER: God had something to say to all our problems. He has so many words of guidance and peace for us. Looking at the manger seems to have so much more meaning for me.

JILL: Thank You, Jesus, for coming and bringing us peace.

SONG: "From Heav'n Above to Earth I Come" *(Joyful Sounds,* Concordia Publishing House)

Recessional

A Traditional Christmas

Diane Gibson

Characters
Mother
Father
Son
Daughter
Mail Carrier
Two children bearing food and gifts
Carolers
Speakers—as many as needed

Setting: A living room with several chairs, a table, a fireplace or wall backdrop with a window.

Props: a newspaper, fabric with sewing needle and thread, a game, matches, Advent wreath with three purple candles and one pink candle, Christmas cards, wrapped Christmas gifts, a plate of wrapped cookies, several white candles, bells, evergreens, holly, a holly wreath, poinsettia plants, a nativity scene, a Christmas tree with lights and ornaments.

Costumes: Ordinary clothes for father, mother, son and daughter; a mail carrier's uniform.

Preliminary Music

Processional Hymn: "O, Come, All Ye Children" (Christian V. Schmid and Johann Abraham Peter Schulz, from *The Children's Hymnal*, Concordia Publishing House)

Invitation to Worship
LEADER: In the name of the Father, and of the Son, and of the Holy Spirit.
CONGREGATION: Amen.
LEADER: Unto us the Christ is born.
CONGREGATION: Oh, come, let us worship Him.

LEADER: Behold, I bring you good tidings of great joy which shall be to all people.

CONGREGATION: For unto you is born this day in the city of David, a Savior, which is Christ the Lord.

LEADER: The Word was made flesh and dwelt among us.

CONGREGATION: Full of grace and truth.

LEADER: Thanks be to God for His inexpressible Gift!

CONGREGATION: Glory to God in the highest, and on earth peace, good will toward men.

A Traditional Christmas

Scene 1—Advent

A family is gathered in the living room. Father is reading the paper, mother is sewing, and the children are playing a game. Father puts down the paper.

FATHER: Son, will you get the matches, please. It's time for our Advent devotions.

SON: Dad, why do we celebrate Advent anyway?

FATHER: During Advent we prepare for the "coming" of the Savior. We look forward to the birth of Jesus. We prepare for Christmas by thinking about our sins and repenting of them. We believe that Jesus came to forgive our sins and we wait eagerly for the second coming of the Savior.

DAUGHTER: But why do we have a wreath with four candles on it?

FATHER: The wreath is a custom that helps us prepare ourselves. Being in the shape of a circle, the wreath stands for eternity, time without end.

MOTHER: The evergreens stand for eternal life in Jesus. The candles represent Jesus as the Light of the world and marks the four weeks of Advent.

SON: Do the colors have any special meaning?

FATHER: The color purple represents the penance and sorrow we feel because of our sins. The first candle reminds us of the prophecy of Jesus coming as a baby in Bethlehem.

MOTHER: The second candle reminds us to give thanks for Bethlehem and for His coming to our community just as God promised.

FATHER: The third candle reminds us to share the good news of Christ's coming, just as the shepherds did.

DAUGHTER: But what about the pink candle?

MOTHER: The pink candle is lit during the last week of Advent. It stands for the joy we have as we wait for Jesus to come.

(The family gathers around the wreath as they light the candles.)

SON: O God, thank You for coming for us at Christmas. Help us to prepare our hearts by repenting of our sins and knowing that You have forgiven them all. We look forward to you coming again. Amen.

SONG: "O Come, O Come, Emmanuel"

Scene 2—Christmas Cards

MAIL CARRIER: Good morning! You received a lot of Christmas cards today! Merry Christmas!

DAUGHTER: Thank you, Mr. Smith. Merry Christmas to you, too. *(She walks into the living room.)* Here are some more Christmas cards, Mom. I wonder how the tradition of the sending of Christmas cards got started.

SPEAKER 1: Long ago school children would make cards called Christmas pieces.

SPEAKER 2: Each child received a piece of paper decorated with a picture from the Bible at the top, and a design around the edges. They would write in the middle with their best handwriting and show them to their parents for approval.

SPEAKER 3: They would often write a Christmas greeting on it and promise to be good.

SPEAKER 4: The first formal Christmas card was designed by an Englishman named J.C. Horsley in 1843 for his friend Sir Henry Cole. It showed a group of grown-ups and children making a toast with the words "A Merry Christmas and a Happy New Year" on it. He printed 1,000 of these cards for Sir Henry Cole who sent them to his friends and relatives.

SPEAKER 5: Today we are so excited about the joys of Christmas that we want to share our joy with others, too.

SPEAKER 6: Today we send cards to wish our friends the happiness we feel because Jesus came for us many years ago.

SONG: "Jesus, Our Good Friend" (Carol Greene and Charlotte

15

Mitchell, from *The Little Christian's Songbook,* Concordia Publishing House)

RECITATION: Jesus is my special Friend. *(point to Heaven)*
　　　　He loves and keeps me to the end. *(point to self)*
　　　　He comes into my heart today. *(cross arms)*
　　　　Oh, won't *you* let Him come to stay? *(point to audience)*

Scene 3—The Giving of Gifts

Two children come to the door bringing gifts and cookies. They hand them to the mother.

FIRST CHILD: Merry Christmas, Mrs. Jones. These are for you from our family.

SECOND CHILD: And these are for you from me. I made them all by myself!

MOTHER: That was very nice of you! Thank you very much! And a Merry Christmas to you, too!

DAUGHTER: I think I know why we exchange gifts. Is it because of the gifts the wise men brought to the baby Jesus?

MOTHER: Well, that is partly why. But gift-giving has some other interesting beginnings as well.

SPEAKER 1: The Romans had two festivals where they gave gifts of twigs from a sacred grove.

SPEAKER 2: These twigs were good luck emblems.

SPEAKER 3: Soon, instead of giving twigs they gave food, candles, statues of gods, and jewelry.

SPEAKER 4: The early church wouldn't accept this practice because they said it was pagan.

SPEAKER 5: But the people enjoyed exchanging gifts so much that they looked to the wise men and explained how *they* brought gifts to Jesus.

SPEAKER 6: Later other respected people such as St. Nicholas gave gifts, so that by the Middle Ages, gift-giving was accepted.

SPEAKER 7: Today as Christians we look upon Jesus as God's special gift to us.

SPEAKER 8: In remembrance of the gift of Jesus to us, we give gifts to others today.

RECITATION: I love you, baby Jesus!
   You are my best present!
   Thank You for coming today!
   Thank You for coming at Christmas!

SONG: "Away in a Manger"

Scene 4—Candles

The family puts candles in the window and on the tables and lights them.

SPEAKER 1: Light was always an important part of the pagan midwinter festivities.

SPEAKER 2: This was because in the winter the people were especially thankful for the warmth and light the sun gave.

SPEAKER 3: To imitate the sun many candles and bonfires were used.

SPEAKER 4: They were suppose to help drive away the forces of cold and darkness.

SPEAKER 5: But to Christians, candles took on a different meaning—of Jesus being the Light of the world.

SPEAKER 6: The practice of putting lighted candles in the windows is believed to have come from Ireland.

SPEAKER 7: At one time the people could not worship God freely and so they weren't allowed to have churches.

SPEAKER 8: The priests would hide in caves and in the forests and would have to visit the farms and homes secretly at night.

SPEAKER 9: The priests would hold a church service for the people in their homes.

SPEAKER 10: Every Irish family hoped that at least once in their lifetime the priest would come to their home on Christmas.

SPEAKER 11: So at Christmastime they kept their doors unlocked and burned candles in the windows so that a priest would be welcomed and guided to their home in the dark night.

RECITATION: Jesus came to be our light
   Just like the candle in the night.
   He lights the way to get to Heaven
   So we can live with Him forever.

SONG: "God Loves Me Dearly" (August Rische, from *Joyful Sounds*, Concordia Publishing House)

Scene 5—Bells

Bells play in the background.

DAUGHTER: There are the church bells ringing again.

SON: There seems to be so many bells ringing at Christmas.

DAUGHTER: Even at the shopping malls there are people standing outside the doors ringing bells.

SON: And many Christmas songs tell about bells, also.

SPEAKER 1: Bells also began with pagan midwinter celebrations.

SPEAKER 2: To the pagan people, evil spirits were very powerful during the cold, dark winter.

SPEAKER 3: One of the ways to drive them away was by making a great deal of noise.

SPEAKER 4: Since making a lot of noise was also a lot of fun, this became an important part of the celebrations.

SPEAKER 5: Bells were good noisemakers because you could shout or sing and ring a bell at the same time.

SPEAKER 6: Today bells are used, not to drive away evil spirits, but to welcome in the spirit of Christmas.

SONG: "Christmas Bells" (Helen Friesen, from Shining Star Publications)

Scene 6—The Plants and Evergreens of Christmas

Children and parents string evergreens and holly, hang a holly wreath, and place several poinsettias in the living room.

SON: Every Christmas we decorate with holly and poinsettias and other evergreens.

DAUGHTER: I wonder if there's some reason for that, too.

SPEAKER 1: Evergreens have been used from ancient times because they symbolize everlasting life.

SPEAKER 2: The use of holly and other evergreens goes back to the time of the Teuton people.

SPEAKER 3: They placed holly and evergreens in their homes in late December to ward off bad weather and evil spirits.

SPEAKER 4: Holly has become especially significant at Christmas. Its red berries signify the red drops of blood Christ shed for us.

SPEAKER 5: The thorns of the holly remind us that Jesus was born to wear a crown of thorns.

SPEAKER 6: The poinsettia is a plant that grows in Mexico and South America. A man named Dr. Joel Poinsett went to Mexico as a U.S. Ambassador. He brought the poinsettia back with him in 1829.

SPEAKER 7: The red flower resembles the star of Bethlehem.

RECITATION: The holly and the evergreen remind us of God's love.
He sent His Son to die for us and shed His precious blood.
He wore a crown of thorns upon His loving, tender head.
For this we thank Him evermore to do this in our stead.

SONG: "The Holly and the Ivy" (Ardis Music Publishing, Inc.)

Scene 7—The Nativity Scene

FATHER: Who would like to help set up the nativity scene this year?

DAUGHTER: Oh, I would! I love to arrange the baby Jesus and Mary and Joseph.

SON: I always like to imagine that I was one of the wise men or one of the shepherds.

MOTHER: I wonder how long ago people started having the nativity scene in their homes?

SPEAKER 1: St. Francis of Assisi started the idea of the nativity scene, or creche, as it is called.

SPEAKER 2: He was a very gentle man, known for his love of animals.

SPEAKER 3: He wanted the people to feel closer to Jesus and realize more clearly how Jesus came to be a man for them.

SPEAKER 4: During his day the church told people that life was sinful and sad.

SPEAKER 5: St. Francis wanted the people to feel the joy and love that the baby Jesus brought at Christmastime instead of sadness.

SPEAKER 6: He wanted people to see with their own eyes how Jesus was born in a humble stable.

SPEAKER 7: So in 1224 he made a life-sized manger with live animals. The people sang carols around it.

SPEAKER 8: The people felt much closer to Jesus when they saw this nativity scene. It made the message of Christmas more real to them.

SPEAKER 9: Today we have creches in our homes to remind us of how Jesus comes into our homes to live.

SPEAKER 10: The creche reminds us of that first Christmas when Jesus came for us.

SONG: "In a Little Stable" (H. W. Gockel and E. W. Schroeter, from *Little Ones Sing Praise,* Concordia Publishing House)

Scene 8—The Christmas Tree

The family lights the Christmas tree and adds ornaments.

SPEAKER 1: Our modern day Christmas tree goes back to medieval times when people had what was called a Paradise Tree.

SPEAKER 2: In the medieval church, December 24 was Adam and Eve Day. Plays were presented portraying the fall of Adam and Eve.

SPEAKER 3: Then they would act out Christ's birth, showing that Jesus had to come to save man from the sins of the first man.

SPEAKER 4: These plays always displayed a "Paradise tree"— the tree from which Adam and Eve ate when they fell into sin.

SPEAKER 5: This custom became popular in homes as well as on stage, and many German households began to set up their own "Paradise trees" on Christmas Eve.

SPEAKER 6: Popular legend attributes the creation of the first Christmas tree to Martin Luther.

SPEAKER 7: One night as he was out walking he looked up at the starry sky through the branches of the trees.

SPEAKER 8: He was so struck with the beauty of the stars gleaming on the trees that he cut down a fir tree and brought it into his house.

SPEAKER 9: He tied candles to the branches and lit them to show his children how the trees outside had glistened in the starlight.

SPEAKER 10: Today almost every home has a Christmas tree. The joy it brings reminds us of our Savior who came to make our happiness complete.

SONG: "O Christmas Tree"

Scene 9—Carols

DAUGHTER: Oh, Mom, there are carolers at the door.

MOTHER: Oh, wonderful! Let them in!

(Carolers come in and sing around the tree.)

FATHER: Did you know that a carol use to be a dance accompanied by singing? The early medieval carols use to be on any subject—religious or nonreligious. They were very popular among the common people who were not interested in the chants and Latin hymns of the church.

MOTHER: It was St. Francis who may have written the first Christmas carols as we would call them today. Christmas songs were sung around his nativity scene in Italy.

SPEAKER 1: People began putting religious words to the melodies of the carols of the time.

SPEAKER 2: Christmas hymns were also composed. These were written specifically to instruct in doctrine.

SPEAKER 3: Today a carol refers to any joyous Christmas song. It reflects the spirit of happiness and joy of Christmas, spreading the cheer and the love that Jesus brought with His birth centuries ago.

SPEAKER 4: A favorite Christmas carol is "Joy to the World." This was written by Isaac Watts. When he was eighteen he was complaining to his father about the poor, unmetrical hymns in their Anglican hymnal. His father suggested that Isaac write better ones if he thought he could.

SPEAKER 5: Isaac did just that. The people in the church liked it so much that he wrote 222 more for his church. One such hymn was "Joy to the World."

SPEAKER 6: Later the words were set to a tune derived by Dr. Lowell Mason from a theme in Handel's Messiah.

SONG: "Joy to the World"

SPEAKER 1: Another favorite Christmas carol is "Silent Night." This was entirely composed on one Christmas Eve in 1818.

SPEAKER 2: It was written by a man named Joseph Mohr who was the assistant priest at a church in Austria. The dampness from the river close by the church caused rust in the organ. The rust was so bad the organ would not play.

SPEAKER 3: Faced with the prospect of a Christmas Eve service with no music, Mohr wrote the three stanzas of "Silent Night" as we know them today. He gave them to his organist Franz Gruber who set them to music.

SPEAKER 4: That night the hymn was sung in that small church by the choir and accompanied by a guitar.

SONG: "Silent Night"

Scene 10—Conclusion: A Traditional Christmas

DAUGHTER: Dad, we sure learned about some interesting Christmas traditions.

SON: Now they mean a lot more to me.

FATHER: We surely want to hang on to these old customs and traditions. Through them God has a way of strengthening our family ties, bringing us closer to our friends, and even bringing us closer to strangers throughout the world.

MOTHER: Most importantly, they draw us closer to the Savior. They bring our thoughts back to that first Christmas when God gave us Jesus.

DAUGHTER: This year I don't want to just "spend" Christmas or "observe" Christmas. I want to "keep" Christmas. I want to keep it with all its beautiful customs and traditions.

SON: How are you going to "keep" Christmas?

DAUGHTER: Oh, but I'll keep it in my heart. That's where it belongs. That's where I want Jesus to stay and live.

SON: I'm keeping Christmas and its message inside me, too. But do you know what's even neater than that?

DAUGHTER: What's that?

SON: Jesus is keeping me in *His* heart, too!

Closing Song: "Hark! the Herald Angels Sing"

The Wise Man

Dawn Olender

Characters

Mr. Wealthy/Father: dressed in an expensive suit
Mrs. Wealthy/Mother: dressed in a semi-formal dress
Alex/Oldest child (age 12): dressed in nice dress pants, nice shirt and tie.
Jill/Middle child (age 9): dressed in a pretty dress
Rachel/Youngest child (age 6): dressed in a pretty dress
Mr. Poverty/Dad: dressed in old jeans and sweat shirt
Mrs. Poverty/Mom: dressed in an old dress
Mike/Oldest child (age 12): dressed in old jeans and sweat shirt
Donna/Middle child (age 9): dressed in old jeans and sweat shirt
Sandy/Youngest child (age 6): dressed in old jeans and sweat shirt

Setting: Two families are on opposite sides of the stage. Each family is around its Christmas tree. The family on the left is very wealthy; their tree is beautifully decorated. The members of this family are dressed elegantly. There are many gifts under the tree. The family on the right is very poor; their tree is decorated with paper chains. The members of this family are dressed in old clothes. There are only four gifts under the tree.

Scene 1

Lights are only shining on left side of the stage on the Wealthy Family. The right side of the stage, the Poverty Family, is dark, but the family is on stage in a freeze position.

FATHER: It's Christmas Eve! It's time to celebrate our family tradition. Each one of you children may open one gift tonight.
CHILDREN: Yippee! Yea!
FATHER *(hands large gift to Alex):* Here, Son, this is just what you wanted. If you don't like the color, we'll take it back the day after tomorrow and exchange it.

23

ALEX (grabs gift): It better be exactly like the picture in the catalog. (He continues to unwrap it.)

MOTHER (hands gifts to Jill and Rachel): These are for you two darlings. They are the best on the market.

JILL: Well, I should hope so. I hate the cheap imitation stuff. (Jill and Rachel unwrap gifts.)

ALEX (holds up gift): Look here, would ya! I finally got my skateboard. It's about time.

MOTHER: Is it the one you wanted, Dear?

ALEX: It sure is! Exactly like the one in the catalog.

MOTHER: Alex, please be sure to wear knee pads and a helmet when you ride it.

ALEX (sarcastically): Oh sure, Mom. I don't have any stupid knee pads, or a helmet.

FATHER: We'll just have to go and buy you some right after Christmas, Son.

RACHEL (holds up gift): Oh, thank you! I love my new dress!

JILL: All we ever get are dumb old dresses. I'm getting tired of getting the same old thing all the time. A new dress every Christmas Eve.

MOTHER: Your father and I were thinking the same thing, Jill. Our Christmas Eves are getting monotonous. That's why we decided to add a little something extra to this year's tradition. We are going to give you something besides presents.

ALEX: What could be better than presents?

FATHER (hands an envelope to each child): You'll find it in these envelopes.

(Children quickly open the envelopes.)

JILL (excitedly): It's money!

ALEX: Hot dog! I got fifty dollars!

JILL: Me, too!

RACHEL: I can't count how much I got.

MOTHER: You have fifty dollars too, Sweetheart.

FATHER: You may spend your Christmas Eve money any way you choose. Your mother and I want you to start learning how to be responsible with finances. So please remember, it's very important that you spend your money wisely. Do you understand? Spend it WISELY!

(Jill and Alex jump up and down. They yell in excitement as they run off the stage—exit left.)

RACHEL: Thank you for my money. I'll do my bestest to spend it wisely.

(Rachel kisses her parents, and skips off stage. Before she disappears totally, she stops skipping and says to herself, "I wonder what wisely means.")

MOTHER *(opens present given to her by her husband):* It's beautiful! *(Lifts up diamond pendant.)* You're a wonderful husband.

FATHER: Darling, do you think we did the right thing by giving the children money?

MOTHER: Why, of course! They need to start learning how to deal with money sometime.

FATHER: You're right. I just hope they spend it wisely.

(Lights fade out as they exit left.)

Scene 2

Lights are now only shining on the right part of the stage, the Poverty Family. The left side of the stage, the Wealthy Family, is dark.

DAD: Well, it's Christmas Eve. It's time to celebrate our family tradition. But if you open your one gift tonight, like you always do, you won't have anything to open tomorrow for Christmas.

CHILDREN: That's okay. We want to open them tonight. Yippee!

DAD *(hands a gift to Mike):* Here, Son, I hope you like it. You deserve to have a better one, but . . . you know . . . *(Gets choked up.)* things are kinda tough.

MIKE: Dad, you know I understand. *(Hugs dad.)*

MOM *(hands gifts to Donna and Sandy):* Here, girls, I hope you like them. I made them myself.

(Sandy and Donna unwrap their gifts.)

MIKE *(holds up gift):* Thanks a bunch! I now have my very own baseball!

DAD: It's really not a very good one, Mike. It's imitation, not like . . .

MIKE: I don't care, Dad. It's a baseball! It's just what I've always wanted. Thanks!

DONNA *(holds up gift):* Oh, Mom! These dresses for our dolls are so cute! Thank you so much!

SANDY: I love them, Mommy. You're the best!

(Children take turns going over and kissing their parents. Then they exit right.)

DAD *(hands a brown paper bag to his wife):* Here, Sweetheart, I got something for you, too.

MOM *(looks surprised):* Oh, Honey! You know we can't afford presents for each other. We must spend our money wisely. We don't have very much.

DAD: Please, accept this gift. It is the least I can do for you. You've been so understanding.

MOM *(looks in bag and begins to cry):* It's the pretty little apron I admired so much at the store. *(She puts it on and hugs her husband.)* You're a wonderful husband. Thank you.

(Lights fade off.)

Scene 3

Children are all playing outside. They are all bundled up in coats. The Wealthy children are in leather coats. The Poverty children are in old jean jackets. The Wealthy children are fighting over the skateboard. The Poverty children are tossing the baseball back and forth to each other. The Wealthy family is on the left; Poverty family is on the right. After this goes on for about a minute, Donna accidently throws the baseball over Mike's head. It lands in the Wealthy family's yard. Alex picks up the ball, and carries it over to the Poverty family's yard. His two sisters follow behind him. At the same time, the three children of the Poverty family begin walking to recover the ball from their neighbor's yard. The six children meet in the center of the stage.

ALEX *(speaks sternly):* Hey! What's the big idea? You almost hit me with this thing.

DONNA *(speaks nervously):* I'm . . . sorry. It was all my fault. I didn't mean to throw it so hard.

JILL *(laughs):* Girls aren't suppose to play with baseballs anyway.

ALEX: Well, I really wouldn't call this a baseball. It's just some cheap imitation.

MIKE: May I please have it back?

ALEX: Why should I give it to you? You threw it over in MY yard. Since it was on OUR property, it belongs to US now.

JILL: Besides, you're not dressed warm enough to play outside. You better go in before you catch a cold. *(Giggles.)*

SANDY *(begins to cry):* Why are you so mean? That's my brother's only Christmas present. You can't take it away from him.

ALEX: Poor baby! Well, if you want it . . . *(Throws ball.)* go get it.

RACHEL: You mean you only get one gift from your parents?

MIKE: Look, my dad just lost his job because he wouldn't cheat for his boss like he wanted him to do. He's a good dad, and he can't help it if that's all he can afford this Christmas. *(Exits right to get ball.)*

ALEX: Well, excuse us. *(Gets a real sassy tone.)* Don't get sore just because you're so poor. It's not our fault. *(Exits left.)*

JILL: Really, You don't have to get so edgy. Come on, Rachel. *(Exits left.)*

RACHEL: Okay, Jill, I'm coming . . . *(Walks closer to Donna.)* Will you promise to stay right here for a minute? I promise to be right back.

SANDY: Maybe. Why should we?

DONNA *(hugs Sandy):* Now Sandy, we must always be kind to others. That's no way to speak to anyone. *(Turns to Rachel.)* Of course we'll wait. But please, hurry. Sandy is getting cold.

(Rachel runs off stage—exits left.)

SANDY *(begins to cry):* Why were they so mean to us?

DONNA *(hugs Sandy tightly):* I'm really not sure Sandy. Some people are just like that. I know it doesn't seem fair, but . . .

SANDY: But it's Christmas. *(Really begins to cry.)*

(Donna continues to try to console her. Rachel finally arrives. She is carrying her white envelope that she received on Christmas Eve. She hands it to Donna.)

RACHEL: Here ya go. This is for your whole family for Christmas.

DONNA *(looks into envelope):* Oh! Rachel, we can't take this. Our parents would never think of accepting your money.

RACHEL: Please, take it. It's okay. My father told me to spend it wisely. So, this is my chance.

(Rachel runs off quickly before Donna has a chance to say anything else. Exits left.)

DONNA: No! . . . Wait! . . . Rachel, come back!

(Lights fade off.)

Scene 4

The entire stage is now the home of the Wealthy family. Mother Wealthy is knitting. Father Wealthy is reading the newspaper. The doorbell rings. Father Wealthy answers the door.

FATHER: What may I do for you children? Are you selling Christmas candy?

DONNA *(pulls out envelope and hands it to him):* Sir, would you please give this back to Rachel for us?

MIKE: Please tell her we said "thank you." It was a very kind deed, but we could never think of taking it.

(Alex comes into the room.)

ALEX: Well, look who's here. Mr. Welfare and company.

FATHER: ALEX!

ALEX: What are they doing here?

FATHER: They came to return the money we gave Rachel for Christmas.

ALEX: You mean you guys stole money from my sister? I oughta bust you.

FATHER: They say Rachel gave it to them.

ALEX: Yeah. By force.

SANDY: That's not true!

FATHER: Where is Rachel?

MOTHER: She's up in her room, dear.

FATHER: Alex, run up and get her. She'll straighten out this whole thing.

(Alex exits left immediately.)

MIKE: We didn't mean to cause any trouble. We just wanted to give Rachel back her money.

MOTHER: Was your conscience beginning to bother you children?

(Rachel and Alex arrive. Rachel runs over and hugs Donna and Sandy.)

FATHER: Rachel, these kids brought over your money. Can you tell me how they got it?

RACHEL: Sure! I gave it to them.

FATHER: But why, Rachel? I told you how you were to spend your money, and . . .

RACHEL: I know Father, you told me to spend it wisely. Well, I wasn't sure what "wisely" meant at first. But then I remembered the story about baby Jesus.

FATHER: What does that have to do with this?

RACHEL: The "wise" men brought gifts to baby Jesus. So, I thought the word "wisely" must have something to do with giving gifts to people who don't have very much.

FATHER: I see.

RACHEL: The wise men gave gifts to baby Jesus. He didn't have very much. So, I gave a gift to someone I knew who didn't have very much.

MOTHER *(with sniffles):* That's very kind, dear. But . . .

FATHER: But, I have a better idea. Go get my checkbook, Rachel. It's in the bottom drawer of my dresser.

(Rachel exits left.)

FATHER: This Christmas, we're going to start a new tradition. Sharing is an important part of Christmas. We're going to help out one family in need every Christmas. We have done very well this year, but that has not always been true. Mike since your family has had a bad year would your family accept a Christmas gift from us?

(Rachel arrives with the checkbook.)

RACHEL: Great, Father. Are you going to be like the wise men, too?

ALEX: Father, may I help? I would like to be a wise man.

(Reaches out to shake Mike's hand. Lights fade off.)

Quantum Leap Christmas

Barbara J. Ritchey

Characters

Dr. Samantha Deckett, physicist
Al, hologram
Zippi, Computer
Ad Person
Shepherd
Joseph, Mary, Boy
Innkeeper
Newscaster
Shepherds (5)

Narrator
Lambs
Wise men (3)
Herod
Angel
Soldier
Centurion
Choir

This production requires little staging and minimal practice. The main burden of the play is on the two main characters, Sam and Al. Props and costumes are of your chosing, can be minimal or more elaborate.

NARRATOR: Dr. Samantha Deckett is a brilliant quantum physicist who made the mistake of experimenting with time travel. Now she finds herself leaping through time controlled by an unknown supernatural force she has come to believe is the Almighty God himself. Her only contact with her own time is Al who appears as a hologram and cannot be seen by those around Dr. Deckett. Al is aided by a computer from Dr. Deckett's lab called Zippi. Zippi stands for Zero Intelligence Perpetual Problem Instrument. Once Dr. Deckett accomplishes whatever task this unseen power wishes of her, she leaps to another time and place. Tonight, Dr. Deckett has traveled farther through time than ever before, unaware of the importance this one leap may have on all mankind.

(Lights flicker as Sam and Al come on stage.)

SAM *(staggers on stage seeming confused and disoriented):* Al, what happened? That wasn't like any other leap I've ever taken? Where am I?

AL *(walks up from behind Sam):* Sam! Zippi had a hard time finding you. You've leaped back in time over 2,000 years to some obscure village in the Middle East.

SAM: Two thousand years. That's impossible.

AL: Look, that must be the town Zippi locked in on to find you. Maybe we can learn something there.

(Sam and Al walk offstage.)

Bethlehem Technical School Commercial

(Ad person comes on stage looking very professional. Should be carrying brochures or catalog about college.)

AD PERSON: Feel as though you're in a rut? Want to do something more with your life, but just don't know where to get started? Call Bethlehem Technical School now. We'll send you a complete brochure telling you how to start a brand new career. Bethlehem Technical School provides training for temple merchants, scribes, tax collectors, carpenters, sellers of purple and many other fulfilling careers. Here's what one of our graduates from the shepherding program has to say about our training.

(Shepherd joins Ad Man on stage and speaks enthusiastically.)

(1) SHEPHERD: I just couldn't seem to get ahead as a beggar at the city gates. Then I enrolled in Bethlehem Technical School and learned how to be a shepherd. The placement service provided by BTS found me a position in no time and within one season on the job, I was given my own hill on which to tend the sheep. BTS opened a whole new life for me!

AD PERSON: Yes, friends, Bethlehem Technical School can change your life and our placement service is guaranteed. Contact BTS now! Operators are standing by to receive your messenger pigeons. Don't delay your new future another moment. Send your pigeon today.

(Ad Person and shepherd leave stage.)

(During song, box for inn is set up and sign saying NO VACANCY is put in place beside it. Sam and Al stand on other side of sign; Innkeeper climbs into box.)

SONG: "O Little Town of Bethlehem"

(When song is finished. Stage manager plugs in sign. Joseph enters stage and stands next to box.)

JOSEPH: Innkeeper! Innkeeper!

INNKEEPER *(opening peephole in door):* We don't have any more room. Can't you read?

JOSEPH: Please, Sir, wait. My wife is with child and her time is near. Surely you have something?

INNKEEPER: I told you there is no room.

SAM: What about the stable?

INNKEEPER AND JOSEPH: What?

SAM: What about the stable? Surely you can let these people shelter there.

AL: Sam, what are you doing?

SAM: Maybe I've been sent here to find shelter for these people to have the baby in. If that's the case, then I'll be leaping to another time as soon as the Innkeeper agrees.

INNKEEPER: Well . . . I suppose it's all right. But just until you can find someplace else to stay. And don't ask for anything else! The stable is in back. Good night!

(Joseph hurries offstage calling out to Mary that he's found shelter for the night.)

SAM: What does Zippi say? Am I leaping out?

AL: Nope, guess that wasn't it. You're still here.

(Joseph runs back on stage and grabs Sam's arm yelling that the baby is coming. Sam and Al follow Joseph offstage. Innkeeper quietly climbs out of box and also leaves stage.)

SONG: "What Child Is This?"

(Sam and Al come back on stage.)

SAM: Did you see that little guy? There's nothing about being a doctor as rewarding as delivering a baby. What does Zippi say? Is that why I was here, to help deliver that baby.

AL: Zippi's having a hard time getting information about this era. He's trying to track down a legend concerning a baby born during this time, but that's about the best he can do. Something about a star appearing in the sky heralding the birth of a king.

SAM: Like that one?

(Sam and Al look up and offstage as if seeing a bright light in the sky. They leave stage, both still watching the star.)

News Bulletin

(Newscaster comes on stage and reads bulletin.)

NEWSCASTER: We interrupt this program to bring you a special news bulletin. Astronomers have just announced the appearance of a strange new constellation shining in Bethlehem's sky. Experts are now standing on rooftops staring at this unheard of phenomenon trying to ascertain its origin. Unconfirmed reports are also flooding in concerning angels appearing on hilltops and music in the air. Please stay tuned to this station for any further developments. We now return you to our regularly scheduled program.

(During song, props from last act removed. Shepherds assemble on stage.)

SONG: "The First Noel"

SHEPHERD 1: Why did the angels come to us
                Lowly shepherds in the night?

SHEPHERD 2: To tell us only that we must
                Follow a holy, shining light.

SHEPHERD 3: For we are simple tenders of sheep
                Yet these instructions we must keep.

SHEPHERD 4: On a bed of hay, the child we'll find
                Who is to be the Savior of mankind.

(Sam and Al come from back of stage.)

SHEPHERD 5: Have you seen this child we seek
                Sleeping in a stable low and meek.

AL: Sam, they're talking about that baby you helped deliver.

(Sam and Al point behind and the shepherds run offstage in the direction from where the two came.)

SAM: Is that why I'm here? To direct the shepherds to the stable?

AL: No . . . you're not leaping yet.

(Sam and Al follow shepherds offstage.)

SONG: "O Come, All Ye Faithful"

(Joseph and Mary come on stage. When song is finished, lambs crawl onto stage. Teachers dressed as shepherds help get youngsters organized into speaking order.)

LAMBS: Why did angels come to tenders of sheep?
           We know the reason why,
           A promise to us lambs they keep
           No more to bleed and die.

The Savior comes our place He takes,
His blood will pay the price.
God with man a bargain makes
His Son the sacrifice.

SONG: "Away in a Manger" *(Song performed by Lambs.)*

(All lights flicker. Lambs, Joseph and Mary leave stage taking manger with them during flickering. Sam and Al return to stage acting confused.)

SAM: Al, what's going on? We didn't leap did we?

AL: Well, no . . . well, kinda'.

SAM: How can we kinda' leap through time?

AL: Zippi says we've gone ahead in time almost two years but we're still close to the same place as before. He says the king's palace is just over there.

(They leave stage. Ad person comes on stage.)

Rent a Camel Commercial

AD PERSON: Planning a little vacation, but getting bogged down with all the details? Is it time to visit friends and relatives over in Egypt, but can't seem to arrange transportation? Call us at Rent a Camel. We have caravans leaving monthly for all destinations. At Rent a Camel, our motto is "Have Camel Will Travel." Don't delay, send that messenger pigeon today and get your reservations confirmed.

(Ad person leaves stage. During song, Sam and Al go to far side of stage where they watch the following dialogue. Wise men assemble on stage in order of speaking. Herod is on other end.)

SONG: "We Three Kings"

WISE MAN 1: The gift of gold is the gift I bring
A gift that's worthy for the newborn king.

WISE MAN 2: The fragrant oil of frankincense I give
To the king of all kings, long may He live.

WISE MAN 3: The spice of myrrh for the king of the ages
Is the final gift given by the wise, foreign magus.

HEROD: Please, most wise of travelers from far off lands, return to me when you have found this king and tell me where He is so that I may worship Him also.

(They shake hands as if in agreement. Wise men lie down as if to sleep. Herod steps back, center and is joined by Centurion.)

HEROD: They are foolish men! As soon as they find that child and tell me where he is, you kill him. There's no room in a palace for more than one king at a time. Understand?

CENTURION: Understood. *(Salutes Herod and leaves.)*

(Sam and Al speak from their position on far side of stage. Angel comes on stage during their dialogue and stands in center behind sleeping wise men.)

SAM: Al, he just gave orders to kill a baby.

AL: Sam, Zippi says it's the same baby you helped deliver when we first leaped here. Zippi says there's an 82% chance that Herod succeeds in murdering the child before he's two years old.

SAM: We've got to warn those wise men not to tell the king where the baby is.

ANGEL: Once you have found the baby you seek, do not return to this place. Go back to your lands using a different route. King Herod plans to murder the child.

(Angel leaves stage. Wise men awaken, get up and also leave stage.)

AL: Looks like an angel beat you to it.

SAM: So why am I here? I'm not here to help them find shelter, I'm not here to deliver the baby, I'm not here to give the shepherds direction, I'm not here to redirect the wise men. The kid's got angels protecting him. Why am I here?

(Herod and Centurion return to stage and stand in center.)

HEROD: Centurion! Those fools have dared to defy me. Assemble your men and go throughout all the land killing any male child you find under the age of two. GO!

(They leave stage.)

AL: Sam, this doesn't look good. Zippi says there's a 94% chance those soldiers find that baby and kill him, tonight!

SAM: We've got to warn his family to get out of the country.

(Sam and Al leave stage.)

Roman Army Commercial

SOLDIER: Caesar Augustus wants YOU! The few, the proud, the Roman Army!

(Soldier marches offstage. Sam and Al return.)

SAM: This is unbelievable. We get there just in time to hear another angel telling Joseph to take his family to Egypt. Another angel! Al, why am I here?

(Joseph, Mary and small child come up behind Sam. All are carrying parcels.)

JOSEPH: Tell me, friend, which road do I take to Egypt?

(Sam looks to Al who consults Zippi and then points to aisle leading to foyer. Sam directs Joseph to follow that route. The family leaves stage and walks down aisle and disappears into foyer. As they walk away one parcel is left behind. Sam and Al watch them depart. Centurion and soldiers rush up behind Sam. Angel returns to far opposite side of stage, stands on chair and points in direction that Joseph and family took.)

CENTURION: Tell me, Jew, did you see a man, woman and child pass by here?

SAM: What man, woman and child?

CENTURION *(picking up article dropped by family)*: We know they came this way, Jew. Which road did they take?

SAM: Which road?

CENTURION *(puts hand on sword and speaks in a threatening manner, other soldiers also act ready to draw swords)*: Tell me which road did the family take?

(Sam hesitates, looks at angel, looks toward aisle family took and then back to angel. Points to same aisle Joseph and family took.)

AL: Sam! What are you doing? You just told them where the boy is. They'll kill him!

CENTURION *(takes hand off sword and other soldiers also relax)*: Your foolish courage is wasted this night, Jew, still I'll spare your life. But your lies do not deceive me. Men! Follow the road to the right, quickly!

(Centurion and guards run down different aisle and exit.)

AL: Sam, how did you know that he wouldn't believe you?

SAM: An angel told me?

AL: You did it, Sam! Zippi says the family makes good their escape to Egypt and the boy survives.

SAM: Does Zippi know what happens to Him?

AL: Zippi says the stable, the star, the shepherds, the wise men and finally this flight into Egypt confirms that this child was believed to have been the Son of God. He grows up, gets a bunch of followers and . . . is murdered at the age of thirty-three.

SAM: He's murdered!

AL: Yeah, public officials stage a mock trial and the mob crucified Him.

SAM: So what's the purpose of everything we just did? What difference does it make whether the child died at the age of two from a soldier's sword or whether he's crucified at the age of thirty-three?

AL: According to Zippi, he's the cause of a religious revolution called Christianity. Legend says that three days after the crucifixion, He was seen walking all over the countryside. His followers claimed He'd risen from the dead. Those thirty-one years made all the difference in the world.

SAM: So if He's the Son of God, then why was I here. He didn't need me, He had angels protecting Him, remember? Why did HE *(Points upward.)* send me here?

AL: Maybe He just wanted you to believe.

SAM: Believe what?

AL: That it isn't a legend. That He really is the Son of God.

(Sam and Al walk offstage. Once out of sight, Al's voice is heard.)

AL: It's time to take another leap, Sam.

SAM: Suppose we ought to change the name of this to Quantum Leap of Faith?

(Characters assemble on stage for closing hymn.)

CLOSING HYMN: "Silent Night! Holy Night!"

BENEDICTION

God's Choice

Millie Barger

Cast of Characters
Beth and Ann: Two women narrators
Man with deep voice for prophecy *(speaks from offstage)*
(Optional—adults, teens or children for these cast members)
Mary
Angel Gabriel
Joseph
Baby Jesus
Young child Jesus
Elizabeth
Innkeeper
Angel
Shepherds
Wise men
Choir
Soloist *(optional)*

Scriptures not identified as from the *King James Version* are from the *New International Version.*

Opening: Downstage (nearest audience)—two women (Narrators/commentators)—in modern-day clothing walk on from opposite sides of platform and stop to talk to each other. Spotlight follows them. They move to left side of stage as they talk. Whenever they refer to action, they turn backs to audience and watch players. Spotlight moves to players.

BETH *(with script in hand):* Hi, Ann, how's it going? Are you ready for Christmas?
ANN: Hi, Beth. *(Gloomily.)* No, I can't seem to get excited about the season this year.
BETH: Hey, what's wrong?
ANN: Well, for one thing, our Christmas program. I wish we could come up with something different from last year. I don't

mean there was anything wrong with it, but it seems that every year the Christmas story is presented the same old way.

BETH *(enthusiastically):* You know, I've been thinking the same thing! And I have an idea. Why don't we take a different look and make the story come alive by showing how things *might* have happened.

ANN: What do you mean?

BETH: Well, I've been using my imagination along with what the Scripture tells us and I've come up with this script. *(Offers one to Ann who opens it and reads as Beth speaks.)* Have you ever wondered about Mary? Why did God choose her to be the mother of the Messiah?

ANN *(looks up):* No, I never thought about it. But when you consider the thousands of young Jewish girls, it makes you wonder. Why do you think He picked this particular one?

BETH: Remember the Old Testament prophecy?

MAN *(deep voice offstage proclaims):* "Behold, a virgin shall conceive, and bear a son, and shall call his name Immanuel" (Isaiah 7:14, King James Version).

ANN: Yes, I remember that. And the Jewish people knew those words. Hebrew parents cherished and protected their young girls. Maybe each family secretly hoped their daughter would be the one honored to bear the holy child.

BETH: But God singled out Mary who lived in Nazareth, a little town in Galilee. Known for her purity, Mary was pledged to be married to a man named Joseph.

ANN: I still wonder, why Mary? There were so many other virgins in Israel. Her purity was not reason enough for God's selection. As the favored one, what other qualities did she have? For instance, how did she react to the angel's message.

BETH: Let's go back in time, and taking into account what the Scriptures tell us, review the scene as it might have happened. *(They consult their scripts.)*

(While they are talking, Mary, dressed in simple straight gown, with uncovered head, enters and sits in shadows. Angel appears facing Mary as Beth speaks.)

BETH: The angel Gabriel, sent by God, appeared to Mary—not to her whole family or to the neighborhood—but to Mary in a quiet place. She may have been in a summer house or in a garden, but she was alone. The angel spoke to her—

(Spotlight on angel.)

GABRIEL: "Greetings, you who are highly favored! The Lord is with you" (Luke 1:28).

ANN *(as angel speaks, spotlight includes Mary whose actions follow the words)*: Mary is astounded and greatly troubled by his words. Dark eyes wide with shock, she stands with trembling hands clasped. All her life she had known this would happen to someone, somewhere, sometime. . . . Now, it is happening to her!

GABRIEL: "Do not be afraid, Mary, you have found favor with God. You will be with child and give birth to a son, and you are to give him the name Jesus" (Luke 1:30, 31).

MARY *(breathlessly, in awe):* The Messiah!

GABRIEL *(nodding):* "He will be great and will be called the Son of the Most High" (Luke 1:32).

MARY: "How will this be, since I am a virgin?" (Luke 1:34).

GABRIEL: "The Holy Spirit will come upon you, and the power of the Most High will overshadow you. So the holy one to be born will be called the Son of God" (Luke 1:35).

MARY *(bowing her head in submission):* "I am the Lord's servant. May it be to me as you have said" (Luke 1:38).

(The angel leaves. . . . Light fades, Mary leaves. Spotlight on narrators.)

BETH: Mary's asking, "How can this be?" gives us another clue to her character. Rather than expressing doubt, her question showed her openness, her transparency, her honesty and her understanding of certain facts of life.

ANN *(nods in agreement):* You're right. In her day, girls did not have babies until they were married. It was natural for her to wonder about how this event could happen.

BETH: I have another question for you. How do you think Mary's parents reacted to her news?

ANN: First of all, I imagine they questioned her. The Scripture doesn't tell us whether they were upset and doubtful or whether they immediately rejoiced with her; but they knew their daughter and they knew the prophecy.

BETH: Also, no doubt the Lord prepared them to believe her. I think they felt deeply honored and blessed to have their daughter chosen to bear the Messiah.

ANN: Do you suppose Mary sometimes wondered if she had dreamed the whole thing, or was she assured and happy?

BETH: To answer that, let's refer to her visit with Elizabeth in a town in the hill country of Judah. *(Elizabeth enters and is seated. Spotlight on her.)* The angel had told Mary of her cousin who for years had wanted a child and was now six months pregnant. When Mary arrived at Elizabeth's house here's what happened.

(Mary enters.)

MARY: Greetings, Cousin Elizabeth.

(Elizabeth rises and with hands on her stomach replies.)

ELIZABETH *(loudly):* "Blessed are you among women, and blessed is the child you will bear!" (Luke 1:42). *(Holds out arms to Mary and they exchange hugs. Elizabeth continues.)* "But why am I so favored, that the mother of my Lord should come to me?" *(Again holds her stomach with her hands.)* "As soon as the sound of your greeting reached my ears, the baby in my womb leaped for joy" (Luke 1:43, 44).

MARY *(joyfully—either speaking or singing The Magnificat):* "My soul glorifies the Lord and my spirit rejoices in God my Savior, for he has been mindful of the humble state of his servant. From now on all generations will call me blessed, for the Mighty One has done great things for me—holy is his name" (Luke 1:46-49).

(Spotlight follows as Mary and Elizabeth leave stage then moves to narrators who face audience.)

BETH: Mary stayed with Elizabeth about three months, then returned to her home.

ANN: What about Joseph? How did he fit into God's plan?

(Spotlight on Joseph who enters, paces back and forth, kneels and prays, then lies down and sleeps. Spotlight back to narrator.)

BETH: Joseph's family line is traced through David back to Abraham. In Matthew's gospel he is described as a just man. When he learned of Mary's condition during their year of engagement, he must have been deeply hurt.

ANN: Apparently he doubted Mary's story of the angel.

BETH: Wouldn't that be natural?

ANN: Of course. And Joseph had to decide what to do about Mary.

(Narrator turns to look at Joseph. Spotlight on angel who stands beside Joseph and speaks.)

ANGEL: "Joseph son of David, do not be afraid to take Mary

home as your wife, because what is conceived in her is from the Holy Spirit. She will give birth to a son, and you are to give him the name Jesus, because he will save his people from their sins" (Matthew 1:20, 21).

(Angel leaves and after a moment Joseph awakens with a smile on his face, yawns, stretches and leaves stage.)

BETH: There was no doubt in Joseph's mind after that. He obeyed the Lord and took Mary into his home but they did not live as husband and wife until after Jesus was born.

ANN *(turns page of script):* I can't wait to see what might have taken place between them.

(Mary and Joseph enter.)

JOSEPH: Mary, you were promised in marriage to me and I was deeply grieved to learn of your condition. Because of my love for you I didn't want to make anything public and I thought of dismissing you privately, until last night.

MARY: I understand, Joseph, but . . .

JOSEPH: No, no! *(Raises both hands, palms toward Mary to shush her.)* Listen to what happened to me last night. As I was sleeping, an angel told me you are the special one chosen to bear the Messiah and that I should not be afraid to marry you.

MARY *(clasps hands together):* Did he really? Oh, Joseph, I'm so glad!

JOSEPH: And Mary, God has given me the privilege of caring for you. I will be honored to take you into my home but we will not live as husband and wife until the Holy One is born.

(As they leave stage, spotlight moves to narrators.)

BETH: Mary trusted God and she trusted Joseph to care for her during her months of waiting for the birth of Jesus.

CHOIR: "Trust and Obey" *(Choir or soloist, visible if room near platform, sings softly first verse and chorus.)*

ANN: From what we've seen and heard, so far, I'm beginning to get an insight into why God chose Joseph and Mary; but I'd like to know more about them.

BETH: Fair enough. Let's go back again to events leading up to the birth of Jesus and listen to Mary and Joseph.

(Mary and Joseph enter, dressed for travel—Mary wears head covering and concealing cloak or shawl.)

JOSEPH: This will be a long, hard trip for you, Mary. I'm sorry it had to come now but we can't disobey the order from Caesar Augustus to report to Bethlehem.

MARY: It is God's will, Joseph. Remember the prophecy?

JOSEPH *(nodding):* Ah, yes, "But you, Bethlehem, in the land of Judah, are by no means least among the rulers of Judah; for out of you will come a ruler who will be the shepherd of my people Israel" (Matthew 2:6).

MARY: That's where Messiah will be born, in Bethlehem. I've prepared swaddling clothes *(Displays bundle.)* to take along and I know the journey will be tiring, but God will provide strength.

JOSEPH: Come, then, let us go.

(They exit.)

CHOIR: "O Little Town of Bethlehem"

(While choir sings, set stage with triple scenes—Inn on right, stable in center, shepherds on hillside on left.)

BETH: The journey to Bethlehem must have tested Mary's strength as she jolted and swayed on the back of a donkey. Joseph made her as comfortable as possible when they camped overnight along the way with other travelers. Finally they arrived in the city and pushed their way through the crowds to an inn.

(Spotlight on inn as Joseph and Mary arrive.)

JOSEPH: Here we are at last, Mary. Tonight you will sleep well in a room with a warm, soft bed.

(Knocks on door of inn.)

INNKEEPER *(sticks head through partially opened door):* It's late, Friend, what do you want?

JOSEPH: A room for the night.

INNKEEPER: I'm sorry, we have no rooms left. You'll have to camp in the streets with the other travelers.

JOSEPH: But my wife's time is near and she must have privacy.

INNKEEPER: Oh, I am sorry. *(Starts to close door then reopens it.)* Wait! There is one place. You may not want it but there's room in the stable. You can spread clean hay to make a bed and at least you'll have privacy.

JOSEPH: Thank you. We'll take it.

(Joseph and Mary move to center stage. Mary sinks to bed of hay or onto floor with her bundle of swaddling clothes. Turn off spotlight as Choir sings softly "Away in a Manger." Then back on to reveal Mary and Baby. Mary follows actions narrator describes.)

CHOIR: "Away in a Manger"

BETH: Mary places her baby diagonally on a square cloth, turns two corners across his body, one across the feet and the other under his head. She then winds strips of cloth around Him to hold the wrappings in place and lays him in a manger.

(Spotlight moves to shepherds and choir sings, "While Shepherds Watched Their Flocks." Angel appears in spotlight and speaks to frightened men.)

CHOIR: "While Shepherds Watched Their Flocks"

ANGEL: "Do not be afraid. I bring you good news of great joy that will be for all the people. Today in the town of David a Savior has been born to you; he is Christ the Lord. This will be a sign to you: You will find a baby wrapped in cloths and lying in a manger" (Luke 2:10-12).

CHOIR *(voices sing or speak):* "Glory to God in the highest, and on earth peace, good will toward men" (Luke 2:14, King James Version).

(Angel leaves.)

SHEPHERD: Let us hurry to Bethlehem and see if we can find the baby. Then we will know this really happened as God made it known to us.

(Shepherds move to stable over which bright light shines.)

ANN: Are we going to see the usual stable scene?

BETH: Maybe, but concentrate on Mary. One of the most revealing signs of Mary's character appears in the visit of the shepherds. Remember, we have wondered why God chose her rather than some other young girl.

(Shepherds excitedly pantomime telling of angel's news, then kneel at manger as choir sings second stanza of "Silent Night! Holy Night!")

CHOIR: "Silent Night! Holy Night!" *(Second stanza.)*

ANN *(in hushed voice):* Mary stayed quietly in the background. She never acted proud or tried to become the center of attention with her baby. She listened and watched the faces of the shepherds. Their awed expressions confirmed what she already knew—this Holy Child was God's gift to all people, to save them from their sins.

(Shepherds hurry down aisles telling news to every stranger they meet. One knocks on door of inn and tells Innkeeper the news. He hurries to the stable.)

INNKEEPER: If I had only known. . . . *(Shakes his head.)* This is

terrible to have such a special one born in a stable. *(Turns to speak to Joseph and Mary.)* I must find you a house.
(Hurries out. Spotlight to narrators. All players leave.)
ANN: Oh, come on, now. Everyone has always thought the innkeeper was a mean old man for not giving them a room that night.
BETH: I'm not so sure about that. He could have been a decent fellow; just helpless with all the rich and powerful people making demands on him. Let's give him the benefit of a doubt.
CHOIR: "O Come, All Ye Faithful"
(As song ends narrators move to center front stage. As they talk, remove scenery and set up house interior.)
ANN: To get back to Mary. She could have talked about the miraculous events in her life up to this point. She could have bragged about this supernatural baby and her part in His appearance on earth.
BETH: Instead, she quietly stored away in her memory everything that happened at this time and meditated on it in the months and years that followed.
ANN: Do you think the innkeeper knew this baby was the Messiah?
BETH: I don't know. I think he must have realized something from the shepherd's story and wanted to make amends. And you know, the news kept spreading. Can you imagine how old King Herod reacted when he heard wise men from the East were in Jerusalem asking about a new king of the Jews?
ANN: Yes. *(With hands behind her back, Ann paces in a small circle as she speaks.)* I can see him pacing the floor in worry over the rumors. He called in all the chief priests and educated men and asked them where the Christ was to be born.
BETH: After he learned the prophecy about Bethlehem, he sent secretly for the wise men and asked them the exact time the star appeared. Then he sent them to Bethlehem to find the child.
ANN: I can see his hypocritical smile as he tells them, *(Ann smiles widely and clasps hands piously in imitation of Herod.)* "As soon as you find him, report to me, so that I too may go and worship him" (Matthew 2:8). *(Ann taps herself on the temple with one finger.)* But in the back of his wicked mind, already he was making plans to kill Jesus.

BETH: Have you ever wondered how long it took the wise men to reach Bethlehem?

ANN: From the time the star first appeared and they traveled to Jerusalem, it might have been several months. I know they didn't travel by jet or Amtrak and even making plans for that long a trip took awhile. I can just see a caravan of camels bouncing along; you know, with servants and all.

BETH: The time element is hinted at when the Scripture says, *(Reads from script.)* "On coming to the house, they saw the *child* with his mother Mary" (Matthew 2:11).

ANN: Yes, I think the innkeeper or someone found a house for the family right away.

(While narrators speak, Mary enters with child under two years of age and holds him on her lap.)

BETH: Well, Ann, you're really getting into the spirit of this play. *(She consults her script.)* And Joseph probably took up his carpentry work there, temporarily.

ANN: Wasn't that fantastic the way the star went before the wise men; and how they were guided to the right house?

BETH: Of course we know it was God's leading. I wonder how Mary felt when those men appeared with their gifts?

ANN *(looking at script):* The scene is set. Let's watch.

WISE MEN *(sing):* "We Three Kings"

(Spotlight on wise men bearing gifts. They come down center aisle singing "We Three Kings" and present their gifts to the Christ child, kneeling as they do so, then exit. After they have gone, Joseph enters.)

MARY: Joseph, see what wonderful gifts have been given to Jesus?

JOSEPH: Gold, frankincense and myrrh? Who brought them?

MARY: They were wise men from the East who followed the star. They said they talked with Herod in Jerusalem and he sent them to find Jesus. What does it mean, Joseph?

JOSEPH: I'm not sure, but I don't think Herod can be happy about the birth of a new future king.

MARY *(in alarm, holding child close in her arms):* He wouldn't harm Messiah, would he?

JOSEPH: We know God will protect His Son, so we can rest and sleep in peace.

(Joseph, Mary and Child exit. Spotlight on narrators.)

BETH: But God knew Herod's wicked heart. An angel of the Lord appeared to Joseph in a dream. The angel warned Joseph that Herod intended to kill Jesus. He told Joseph to take the child and his mother to Egypt and stay there until Herod was dead.

ANN: Without question, Joseph obeyed God's command and that very night they fled to Egypt. Did Herod find out about that?

BETH: Not likely. When the wise men didn't return to bring him the information he wanted, he was furious and ordered the killing of all boys under the age of two in Bethlehem and the surrounding area. That was a sad, sad time for all the families with young sons. *(Pause, both with heads bowed, then look up and continue.)* So you can see why God chose someone like Joseph who would obey Him instantly in a time of crisis.

ANN: Yes. I understand better now why he chose both Joseph and Mary. But I have another question. Jesus was born in Bethlehem but grew up in Nazareth. How did that happen?

BETH: After Herod died, an angel of the Lord told Joseph in Egypt that Herod was dead and he should take the child and his mother to Israel.

ANN: So they settled in Nazareth and Mary continued to be a good mother to Jesus who grew up helping Joseph in the carpentry shop.

BETH: Right. We'll finish our story with this comment: Never again will God choose anyone for such a special role as Joseph and Mary's *(Pauses, then emphasizes.)* but He *still* seeks lives with potential; that is, people who will give their lives to Him so that He can use them according to His will and His purpose.

ANN: Also, we want to remember that the greatest joy in the world is in knowing and receiving God's gift of His Son.

BETH: Of course. Jesus didn't remain in the carpentry shop but ministered to many people, and then gave His life on the cross for all who will receive Him as Savior.

ANN: I'm glad we've had this time of remembering and imagining events of so long ago and I'm thankful I know Him as my Savior.

BETH: I'm happy to know we can share this good news with others. Let's tell the world!

(They leave stage.)

CHOIR: "Joy to the World" *(This may be sung by everyone.)*

Lights Along the Way

Pearl Hodges

A Christmas Candlelight Service

Personnel and Props:
- One Candlelighter
- Narrator *(speaking from offstage is effective)*
- Arrange for singers or have tapes of the chosen songs to be played.
- Center Stage: A table draped with gold lamé topped with two five-branch candelabra; use ten white tapers.
- One single candleholder holding a tall white taper arranged to sit between the two candelabra. This single taper represents Jesus' resurrection and is last to be lit.
  (An interesting touch is to work the lamé or other regal type fabric into and around the candles. This gives a majestic feel to the entire centerpiece.)
- All house lights are turned off before narrator begins.
- Congregation is provided candles as they arrive. Candles are lit by the candlelighter as designated in the script. **It is most important to remember that the unlit candle is the one tipped to receive the flame, never the lighted candle. Always remember to use fire safety precautions and observe all fire laws.**

All Scripture references are taken from the *Holy Bible, New International Version.*

NARRATOR: Long, long ago, before the beginning of time, there was total darkness. The earth was void of any form. But God, hovering over, said, "Let there be light and there was light."

*(**Light Candle #1** at the phrase "Let there be light.")*

NARRATOR: When He was all finished creating the universe, God made the first man, Adam, and the first woman, Eve, and placed them in the beautiful Garden of Eden. They knew the light of God's presence day and night.

Perfect peace in the garden was interrupted by Satan's temptation to disobey God's one command—and with one bite of the forbidden fruit, the first human sin was committed.

Their hearts, once aglow with God's presence, were now darkened. No more were they innocent and free. They were expelled from the garden to toil and sweat to extract a living from the earth that was, itself, cursed to groan under its load and grow thistles and thorns.

To keep the light of hope alive, God cursed the serpent through which Satan had spoken. To him, God leveled a blow that would be meted out during the course of human history. He said, "I will put enmity between you and the woman, and between your offspring and hers; he will crush your head and you will strike his heel" (Genesis 3:15).

(Light Candle #2 at "he will crush your head.")

NARRATOR: This was the beginning of God's awesome revelation of how He would one day send a Redeemer into the world. This Redeemer would be born of a woman and though Satan would strike his blows, the Redeemer would, in the end, crush Satan's head.

Through the years that followed, God kept the light of hope alive. From Abraham and his descendants, He formed a nation that would be His special people—the vehicle that would usher in this promised Redeemer.

(Light Candle #3.)

NARRATOR: Although men like Jacob and Moses repeated the promise that God would one day send a redeemer, this special nation, Israel, repeatedly rebelled against Him. God continued to show them how desperately man needed a way out. He foreshadowed His redemptive plan by setting in motion rituals of feasts and sacrifices that would ultimately be fulfilled in and through the life, the death, and the resurrection of the Messiah, His son, Jesus Christ. But Israel was a stubborn people; it would take centuries before God's timing would allow for the Messiah's birth.

As time passed, God raised up kings and prophets that urged Israel to follow God closely and watch for the coming Redeemer.

Prophets Jeremiah, Ezekiel, and Zechariah declared that a future king would come from the lineage of David. His birth would herald a new beginning—a new covenant.

It was the prophet Micah who shed light on where this most unusual birth would occur.

"But you, Bethlehem Ephrathah, though you are small among the clans of Judah, out of you will come for me one who will be ruler over Israel, whose origins are from of old, from ancient times" (Micah 5:2).

(Light Candle #4.)

NARRATOR: Prophet Isaiah, seven centuries before Christ's birth, prophesied that the time of darkness and despair would not go on forever. He said, "The people walking in darkness have seen a great light; on those living in the land of the shadow of death a light has dawned" (Isaiah 9:2).

How was this light going to pierce the darkness? It would be just as God had indicated back in the Garden of Eden. Listen as Isaiah continues, "Therefore the Lord himself will give you a sign: The virgin will be with child and will give birth to a son, and will call him Immanuel" (Isaiah 7:14). Immanuel meaning, "God is with us".

Emphasizing that this child would be God's Son, Isaiah states, "For to us a child is born, to us a son is given, and the government will be on his shoulders. And he will be called Wonderful Counselor, Mighty God, Everlasting Father, Prince of Peace" (Isaiah 9:6).

(Light Candle #5.)

SONG: "O Come, O Come, Emmanuel" *(It is effective to have this sung from offstage or have it played on tape.)*

NARRATOR: As though looking down the long corridor of time, Isaiah prophesied that it would be this Prince of Peace that would bring about true liberty even though He would be rejected by His people, silent before His accusers, pierced for our sins, executed between two thieves, buried in a rich man's tomb but resurrected and alive in Heaven as our intercessor.

Malachi was the last prophet to write and he even prophesied that this yet to be born king would one day return to earth and at that time every knee will bow to the Lord of lords.

(Light Candle #6.)

NARRATOR: Four hundred years of silence passed from the time of Malachi. World powers changed several times—Persia, Greece—finally Rome. Life continued with the hope of a Messiah still only a dim light in the future.

Then, in God's perfect timing, He chose a young virgin in the city of Nazareth—her name was Mary. She was engaged to a man named Joseph, a descendant of King David.

God sent the angel Gabriel to inform her that she would give birth to a baby whom He alone had placed within her.

Joseph also was informed of the baby by an angel. He was told that the baby's name would be Jesus and this Jesus would grow up to save His people from their sin.

At last, after centuries of waiting, the light was breaking through.

(Light Candle #7.)

NARRATOR: Well, you know the story, He was born—this baby that had no earthly father; in a cattle feeding trough, of all places. This son of God whose sole purpose was to become a human bridge between sinful man and Holy God, was born. **A Very Strange Way to Save the World**—but that's why He came.

(Light Candle #8.)

SONG: "Strange Way to Save the World" *(Recorded by 4 HIM, 1993, Benson Recording—accompaniment track available. Substitute appropriate song if needed.)*

NARRATOR: Shepherds that night, were no doubt, bedazzled by the brilliancy of angels in the sky proclaiming Jesus' birth. No doubt, the wise men, who later visited the child Jesus, were amazed by the bright star that guided them to Him. But those lights went away. It was the light of Jesus that remained.

Though many would try to snuff out this Light, the fact remained that He was the Light that the prophets had spoken of. He was the one whom God said would crush the serpent's head. He was himself Creator of all things. He had always been alive. Now, He was on earth to become our Savior.

Apostle John said, "In him was life, and that life was the light of men. The light shines in the darkness, but the darkness has not understood it" (John 1:4, 5).

(Light Candle #9.)

NARRATOR: John also records that though He made the world, the world didn't know Him. While many believed, many accused him of being an imposter and an insurrectionist.

He was put to death but the Light was not extinguished; it burned even brighter because God's requirement for blood sacrifices to atone for sin had been satisfied. Jesus had just become the perfect sacrifice.

(Light Candle #10.)

NARRATOR: He was laid in a tomb, but the tomb could not extinguish the Light. That little baby, born so very long ago, who grew to manhood and lived thirty-three perfect years on earth, made the only payment that God will accept for our sin. But He arose from the grave, He paved the way for us to join Him in Heaven when life here is over. The Light of the world, JESUS, replaced fear of death as He walked out of the tomb alive. It was for this moment that He was born.

(Light Candle #11.)

SONG: "A Great Joy" *(As recorded by Babbie Mason, 1992 by Word, Inc.—accompaniment track available. Substitute another song of joy if desired.)*

NARRATOR OR OTHER DESIGNATED PERSON: With light from the candle symbolizing our Lord's resurrection, I come to you with light for your candles. Because Christ lives, we, His children, can shed light in the dark world to those in despair.

(Designated persons light candles of those seated at end of the pews. They in turn light the one next to them and so on.)

SONG: "A Thousand Candles" *(as recorded by Evie Tornquist Karlsson, 1991 Word, Inc.—accompaniment track available. Candles are being lit as song is sung. Substitute another song about light if desired.)*

NARRATOR *(after all candles are lit)*: Lift your candles high for a moment. . . . The glow of Christmas candlelight never grows old does it? Each year we leave with its glow warming our hearts.

You may lower your candles. But consider for a brief moment how dark your life would be if there wasn't the light of hope burning deep within you.

Sharing that light of hope and security would be the best Christmas gift any of us could give back to the one who set the world aglow and whose birthday we celebrate tonight.

Please sing with me "Silent Night! Holy Night!" as our benediction.

SONG: "Silent Night! Holy Night!"

(Candles are extinguished at conclusion of song.)

A Pine Creek Thanksgiving

Michelle M. Lawrence

This play is designed for a classroom or Sunday school production. The size of the cast can be adjusted to suit the needs of the performance. This play demonstrates to children that they can make a difference in the lives of others, especially people that are "different" than themselves.

Characters
Tim Antonelli—about 8 years old
Terri Antonelli—about 10 years old
Mrs. Antonelli—Tim and Terri's mother
Mr. Antonelli—Tim and Terri's dad
Mrs. Caine—an elderly neighbor
Mr. Franklin—a wheelchair bound elderly neighbor
Mr. Valdez—new to America from Puerto Rico
Mrs. Valdez—married to Mr. Valdez—knows very little English
Ricky Valdez—friend of Tim, about 10 to 12 year old
Maria Valdez—younger sister of Ricky, a friend of Terri
Frankie Valdez—preschool brother of Ricky and Maria
Mrs. Jones—pregnant neighbor of the Antonelli's
Mr. Jones—a quiet man, husband of Mrs. Jones
Sarah Jones—about 11 years old
Jones children—5 to 7 children, various ages—no speaking roles

Setting
Scene 1—The supper table at the Antonelli's.
Scene 2—Monday after school in the basement.
Scene 3—A few days before Thanksgiving in the basement.
Scene 4—Thanksgiving day at Pine Creek Apartments.

Props: Scene 1—A kitchen table and four chairs, a real or makeshift sink, a checkers game, plates, silverware and drinking glasses for three people.
Scene 2—Construction paper, pens, scissors.
Scene 3—A couple of brooms, a pail, a mop and sponges.

Scene 4—A long table, enough chairs or stools for everyone attending the feast, place settings for everyone, real or pretend Thanksgiving dishes for the feast, a wheelchair if possible.

Time: The present, about a month before Thanksgiving and up to Thanksgiving Day.

Costumes: No costumes required unless children portray adults in their roles. Someone will have to use a pillow or stuffing to portray a pregnant Mrs. Jones.

Scene 1

TIM: Today in school we listened to a story called the "Green Valley Thanksgiving." It was about a big family with great grandparents, grandparents, aunts, uncles and cousins. They all got together to celebrate Thanksgiving at the big farmhouse that the Miller family lived in. Can you imagine such a big family? I wish we could have a Thanksgiving like that.

TERRI: How could we Tim? We don't have lots of relatives. We don't have any great grandparents or grandparents. We have no aunts and only uncle Steve who lives on the other side of the country.

MRS. ANTONELLI: Besides that, where in the world would we put all those people in this little apartment? Just be grateful that we have each other. Best of all, this year Dad doesn't have to work at the factory on Thanksgiving. We'll all be together. *(Mom clears the table and the children help her take the dishes to the sink.)*

TERRI: I guess we are lucky that we have each other. I haven't seen any people come to visit poor, old Mrs. Caine across the hall in 3B or that old man in a wheelchair in 1A either.

MRS. ANTONELLI: The old man in 1A is Mr. Franklin. His wife died two years ago. He doesn't seem to get many visitors. *(Mrs. Antonelli begins to wash the dishes. The children go to the table and play checkers.)* Come to think of it, the Valdez family in 2B must be pretty lonely since all of their relatives are back in Puerto Rico. They have only been here in the United States for three years.

TERRI: Do you know the Jones family in 1D? They have all those kids and their mother is going to have another baby soon.

TIM: Yeah, and Bobby Jones told me that his dad got laid off work last week.

MRS. ANTONELLI: I guess a lot of people in this building won't be having a very happy Thanksgiving this year.

TERRI: I've got a great idea! Let's have a big Thanksgiving feast for all the people in our building.

TIM: Yeah, we can call it the Pine Creek Apartments Thanksgiving!

MRS. ANTONELLI: It sounds like a great idea Terri, but, there is one problem—where will everyone eat for this feast? All the apartments are too small for that many people to gather together.

TIM: How about the basement? We ride our bikes down there when it rains. There's plenty of room down there.

MRS. ANTONELLI: Tim, you are a genius! *(She hugs both of her children who had walked over to the sink.)* I have great kids who have such wonderful ideas. We will have to rent folding tables and ask everyone to bring their own chairs and place settings. Also, everyone can bring their favorite dishes to share at the feast.

TERRI: I'll make the invitations! I have plenty of construction paper.

TIM: I'll help too!

TERRI: Okay, you can make turkeys to glue to the front of the invitations. Go and tell all the kids in the building about our Thanksgiving feast. Let them know that we are going to meet after school on Monday to pick the songs we will sing for our families. We have almost three weeks, so we can plan a great time.

Scene 2

The children from the apartment building all meet in the basement to plan the Thanksgiving celebration feast.

TERRI: As you all know by now, we are having a big Thanksgiving celebration for everyone in our building. We are having it down here in the basement. My dad checked with the apartment management today and they said that it's okay for us to have it down here.

MARIA: How can we help? It sounds like so much fun!

TERRI: Today we have to make the invitations. Everyone can help. Then we have to deliver them to everyone in the building.

(The children all work together and make the invitations.)

TERRI: Before we all leave today, let's think of some special entertainment for that day.

SARAH: Why don't we sing songs?

RICKY: Yes, let's sing some Thanksgiving songs. I'd love to learn some so that I can teach my family.

TERRI: That's a great idea! We'll sing a couple of songs for our families.

(The teachers or leaders of this play can choose the songs they want their group to sing.)

TERRI: Think about what songs you want to sing and we'll meet down here again next Monday after school. Don't forget the invitations!

(Everyone cleans up the scraps of paper from the invitations; then they all leave together.)

Scene 3

In the basement of the apartment building, Mrs. Antonelli, Mrs. Valdez and their children are cleaning.

MRS. ANTONELLI: I can't believe that Thanksgiving is only three days away

MRS. VALDEZ: Yes, I cannot wait! This is my family's first real Thanksgiving.

TIM: We are going to scrub these floors so clean that they will sparkle!

MRS. ANTONELLI: Mrs. Caine is so excited about coming that she is making pretty place mats for everyone.

MARIA: I can't wait to eat all that great food!

MRS. ANTONELLI: Let's all get busy now so that our "dining hall" will be ready for Thursday.

(The two mothers and their children continue cleaning.)

MRS. ANTONELLI: Now everything is ready for the day of our feast. The tables will be delivered on Wednesday. We'll see you and your family on Thursday! *(Everyone leaves.)*

Scene 4

Everyone in the building enters to come to the Thanksgiving feast. Tim, Terri and Mrs. Antonelli enter first, helping Mrs. Caine by the arm.

TIM: What did you make Mrs. Caine?

MRS. CAINE: I made a crumbtop apple pie, savory black-eyed peas and a big pot of sweet potatoes with lots of brown sugar. When I was growing up in Alabama, my mama always served black-eyed peas and sweet potatoes on Thanksgiving.

TERRI: Your place mats are beautiful Mrs. Caine!

MRS. CAINE: Why thank you child! You children certainly did a fine job decorating this old basement too. It looks like a fancy restaurant! What did your mother make for our feast?

TERRI: She made her famous lasagna and, of course, pumpkin and mincemeat pies.

(Enter Mr. Antonelli and Mr. Valdez with Mr. Franklin in his wheelchair. The rest of the Valdez family follows them.)

MR. FRANKLIN: I sure appreciate you two fellows helping me down here so that I can enjoy this wonderful feast.

MR. ANTONELLI: No problem! We wouldn't want you to miss all of the fun.

(Mr. Franklin is holding two plates of food.)

TERRI: I'll take those for you Mr. Franklin. What did you bring?

MR. FRANKLIN: No Thanksgiving dinner is complete without cranberry sauce and celery stuffed with cream cheese.

MR. ANTONELLI: Sounds delicious. I can't wait to eat!

MRS. VALDEZ: Terri, give these to your mother. We made baked rice with garbanzo beans, and chicken with sofrito sauce.

RICKY: We also brought lots of mashed potatoes and gravy. My sister and brother helped me peel a whole bag of potatoes!

(Terri and Tim help everyone find their seats. Enter the Jones' family. Mrs. Antonelli greets them.)

MRS. JONES: I'm sorry that we couldn't bring more for the celebration, but things have been rough for us lately. All we could bring to share is lots of cornmeal muffins and lots of kids!

(Everyone laughs with Mrs. Jones as the Jones family is seated at the table. Mr. Antonelli stands up to speak.)

MR. ANTONELLI: Listen everyone. Not only did the apartment management agree to let us use this basement for our celebration, they also gave us the three wonderful turkeys that you see in front of us. The turkeys came cooked and ready to eat! I say three cheers for the Pine Creek Apartments management!

(Everyone claps and cheers. Mr. Antonelli sits down and Tim stands up.)

TIM: I say three cheers for our first annual Pine Creek Family Thanksgiving!

(Everyone cheers and claps even louder than before.)

TERRI: Will all the kids please come from the table now, because we are going to sing a couple of songs of thanks and praise.

(All of the children stand and Terri will start them singing. She looks out into the audience and at the adults seated at the table.)

TERRI: We hope that all of you will join in with us.

(At this point, Terri leads the children in singing the songs that were previously chosen by the play director. After the songs, the children turn to the audience.)

CHILDREN: Happy Thanksgiving everyone!

Appreciation Points

Esther M. Bailey

A Thanksgiving Program

Characters
Narrator
Anchor Person
Three Reporters
Three Women to be interviewed; Mrs. Boyd, Brenda Smith,
  Dottie Crane
Three Men to be interviewed; Mr. Drake, Dave Wilcox, John
  Roberts
Note: One person could play more than one part if necessary.

Props: A lectern should be placed on one side of the stage. A microphone with a cord long enough to reach center stage should be available in addition to the microphone at the lectern. A box labeled "We Give Thanks" should be placed on a table in front. Provide slips of paper and pencils.

Time: Thanksgiving Eve

Costumes: regular clothing

NARRATOR: During news coverage of tragic events, a reporter will often interview two persons with different reactions. While one person is totally devastated, someone else may focus on something positive. Let's observe a few typical scenes that show two ways of handling problems.
(Narrator steps away from lectern to have a seat. Anchor person steps to lectern.)
ANCHOR PERSON: Good evening, I'm *(name)* bringing you news from *(the nearest television station).* On this Wednesday evening before Thanksgiving, the news we have to report might suggest any emotion except thanksgiving. Yet some people find what we might call "appreciation points" even in tragedy.

We begin with a story of natural disaster. Along California's coast, an earthquake measuring 7.2 on the Richter scale has once again hit the San Francisco area. *(Names reporter)* is on the scene.

FIRST REPORTER *(walking to center stage with microphone in hand, Mrs. Boyd follows):* The hardest hit area has already been blocked off by officials. I'm standing just outside the barricade where Mrs. Boyd has been stopped in trying to reach her home. Mrs. Boyd, what have you been told to expect?

MRS. BOYD: The worst, really. Homes are in shambles, and we'll be lucky to salvage our belongings.

REPORTER: What will this do to your observance of Thanksgiving?

MRS. BOYD: It will definitely change our perspective. Yet it could have been so much worse. My children could have been here when it happened. Instead, my mother picked them up at school and took them to her house where my husband and I plan to spend Thanksgiving.

REPORTER: Then you will go on with the celebration as usual?

MRS. BOYD: Not exactly. Our loss will be much on our minds, but we'll hold up—especially for the sake of the children. We'll give thanks because we are all safe and we'll look forward to the time when we can get our lives back to normal.

REPORTER: Thank you, Mrs. Boyd and best of luck. *(Mrs. Boyd exits. Mr. Drake enters.)* Mr. Drake also just learned that he has no home to go to. Would you like to express your feelings to viewers, Mr. Drake?

MR. DRAKE: My feelings? To tell you the truth, I feel like crawling to my house and burying myself in the rubble.

REPORTER: Then you won't be celebrating Thanksgiving tomorrow?

MR. DRAKE: I don't have anything to be thankful for.

REPORTER: Do you have family?

MR. DRAKE: My wife should be along any time now, but she'll feel just like I do. We'll never get over this.

REPORTER: I'm sorry, Mr. Drake. I can only hope that time will change things for you.

(Reporter and Mr. Drake exit.)

ANCHOR PERSON: Closer to home, we have more bad news. Employees of Catco Tools Manufacturing Company have just been told that the plant will close as of the first of the year. One hundred eighty-five *(Large metropolitan areas should increase number.)* people will be out of work. *(Names reporter.)* will interview two people as they leave the plant.

SECOND REPORTER *(entering followed by Dave Wilcox):* Dave Wilcox is with me just outside Catco Tools where an announcement has just been made that he will lose his job. Mr. Wilcox, what is your reaction?

DAVE WILCOX: It's just about the end of the world for me. I've hardly been making it without this. Some happy Thanksgiving, I'd say. Guess that's the way rich people are—don't care a thing about the little guy.

REPORTER: Has the company not reported a loss the past two years?

DAVE WILCOX: A loss? What does that mean? After the huge salaries to the big boys I suppose there would be a loss.

REPORTER: You sound like a bitter man, Dave.

DAVE WILCOX: I'm bitter all right. I don't know how anyone could expect me to feel otherwise.

REPORTER: I'm sorry—really sorry. *(Dave Wilcox exits. John Roberts enters.)* I have John Roberts here now. John, you heard what Dave Wilcox had to say. How do you feel about the plant closing?

JOHN ROBERTS: I'm disappointed, of course. It'll be tough on me and my family.

REPORTER: Does it bother you that the company made the announcement on Thanksgiving Eve?

JOHN ROBERTS: The sooner we know the better, I'd say. Then we can start stretching the pay checks.

REPORTER: The news won't affect your holiday celebration?

JOHN ROBERTS: Oh, yes, but we still have much to be thankful for. Everyone in the family is in good health and we'll make out somehow.

REPORTER: That's a very fine attitude, John. I wish you well.

JOHN ROBERTS: Thank you.

(Reporter and John Roberts exit.)

ANCHOR PERSON: On a different note, but still on the subject of bad news, we take you to upstate New York. There, it is estimated that some six hundred chemical workers have been exposed to toxic fumes when a tank containing hazardous materials sprang a leak. Some workers were treated at the hospital and released. The rest were sent home early. *(Names reporter.)* caught two of the workers as they left the plant.

THIRD REPORTER *(walking to center stage with microphone in hand, Brenda Smith follows):* This has been a bad day for Upstate Chemical Company workers. Toxic fumes spewed forth from a tank that sprang a leak. Here to tell us what happened is Brenda Smith.

BRENDA SMITH: All at once we smelled this terrible odor. Then an announcement came over the loud speaker telling everyone to vacate. Some workers nearby the tank were overcome by the fumes and had to be taken to the hospital.

REPORTER: Do you feel any ill effects from the fumes?

BRENDA SMITH: My eyes burn, I have a headache, and I'm coughing. *(Coughs.)*

REPORTER: Will what happened affect your observance of Thanksgiving?

BRENDA SMITH: I'll say it will. I didn't have a lot to be thankful for before this happened. Now I'll probably have cancer to look forward to in a few years

REPORTER: The company spokesperson says that the level of exposure should cause no permanent damage. Does that give you any comfort?

BRENDA SMITH: Not a bit. They'll tell you anything to get out of responsibility.

REPORTER: Thank you, Brenda. I hope your symptoms prove to be temporary. *(Brenda Smith exits. Dottie Crane enters.)* I see Dottie Crane is smiling. Dottie, do you feel threatened by today's happening?

DOTTIE CRANE: I wouldn't use the word "threatened." I'm concerned, but I'm going to try to keep an upbeat attitude. What's happened has happened and I'm going to hope for the best.

REPORTER: You're still going to celebrate Thanksgiving tomorrow?

DOTTIE CRANE: Indeed I will. I believe that being thankful helps us handle whatever comes our way.

REPORTER: Even cancer?

DOTTIE CRANE: Particularly matters of health such as cancer. A positive attitude goes a long way in healing.

REPORTER: I hope your attitude is contagious. Best wishes.

DOTTIE CRANE: Thank you.

(Reporter and Dottie Crane exit.)

ANCHOR PERSON: We'll be back with more news in just a moment.

NARRATOR: These scenes help us to understand why the apostle Paul wrote, "Be joyful always; pray continually; give thanks in all circumstances, for this is God's will for you in Christ Jesus" (1 Thessalonians 5:16-18, *New International Version).*

Bitterness will not relieve any of the grief connected with a bad break, but thanksgiving will. Of course we aren't going to jump for joy when tragedy first strikes. We wouldn't be human if we did. As we analyze the situation, though, we will find some reason to give thanks.

We're going to practice that right now. First, I'd like us to think about the best thing we have going for us—a good job, a good marriage—whatever. On the little sheets of paper *(Explain where they are found.)* write out three things that you appreciate about that situation. *(Allow three to five minutes while music plays softly.)*

Now let's think about the part of our lives that gives us the most concern—a poor report from the doctor, problems with a child. Try to find just one appreciation point in that situation, and write it down.

(Allow three to five minutes while music plays softly.)

As further indication of our thanksgiving to God, we're going to sing a song *(or chorus)* of thanksgiving and place our expressions of thanks in our "Thanksgiving Box" on the table. Let's start on this side *(indicate)* and march around the room. When you drop your list of appreciation points into the box, pause for a moment to allow the gratitude to flow from your heart.

(Close with a prayer of thanksgiving.)